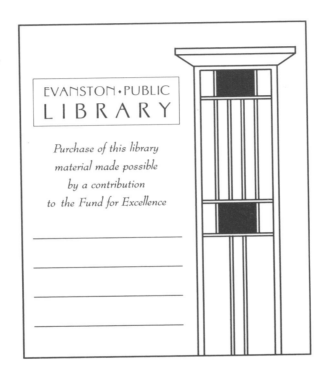

In Touch With Nature
Flowering Plants

**BLACKBIRCH®
PRESS**

THOMSON

GALE

San Diego • Detroit • New York • San Francisco • Cleveland • New Haven, Conn. • Waterville, Maine • London • Munich

PHOTOGRAPHIC CREDITS
Art Explosion: 27, 30tr, 30br; **Art I Need:** 4–5, 28; **Bio-Photo Services Inc:** 3; **Corbis Royalty Free:** 23; **Image ideas Inc:** 1; **Photodisc:** 5r, 6–7, 9, 12, 14, 15, 17, 18–19, 22, 26, 29l; **USDA/ARS:** Peggy Greb 29r, Keith Weller 30l.

Step-by-step photography throughout: Martin Norris

Front cover: Martin Norris and Photodisc

Consultant: Mark Hostetler, Ph.D.,
  Assistant Professor, Extension Wildlife Specialist,
  Department of Wildlife Ecology & Conservation,
  IFAS, University of Florida

For The Brown Reference Group plc
Editorial and Design: John Farndon and Angela Koo
Picture Researcher: Helen Simm
Illustrations: Darren Awuah
Managing Editor: Bridget Giles
Art Director: Dave Goodman
Children's Publisher: Anne O'Daly
Production Director: Alastair Gourlay
Editorial Director: Lindsey Lowe

LIBRARY OF CONGRESS CATALOGING-IN-PUBLICATION DATA

Available from the Library of Congress.

ISBN: 1-4103-0121-4

Printed and bound in Singapore
10 9 8 7 6 5 4 3 2 1

Contents

What are flowers?

Did you know?
The world's biggest flower is the
rafflesia of Southeast Asia. It
grows up to 3 feet
(1 m) across.

To most of us, a flower is a plant with colorful blooms. For scientists, the flower is just the bloom itself. They call any plant that has flowers at some time in its life a flowering plant. Some blooms are big, bright, and hard to miss, like roses. Other plants have flowers so tiny and short-lived, you can easily miss them.

In fact, nearly all plants are flowering plants—not just garden flowers and wildflowers, but every herb, grain, grass, shrub, fruit, and vegetable. Even most trees, like oaks and elms, are flowering plants. There are about 275,000 kinds of plants altogether, and 250,000 are flowering plants. Lichens, mosses, ferns, and certain trees (see Close-up: Trees) are the only plants that are not. The flowers are not just for show. Each bloom contains the parts that create the seeds from which new plants grow. The technical word for a flowering plant—angiosperm—comes from the ancient Greek for "container" and "seed."

Garden flowers and wildflowers

All flowers grew wild originally. Over the centuries, gardeners adapted flowers for the garden. They selected seeds and joined

A field of scarlet
The bright red flowers of poppies have just one purpose: to make seeds.

plants to bring out chosen qualities, such as bright blooms or straight stems. There are now more than a million kinds of garden flower. All these kinds are only variations, not species, however. Gardeners cannot create new species. All they can do is create what are called hybrids. They create hybrids by introducing pollen from one plant to the seeds of another. In the meantime, though, many species of wildflower are becoming very rare as people damage or destroy many of the places plants grow.

CLOSE-UP *Trees*

Trees range widely in size, from dwarf willows a few inches high to vast redwoods as tall as a skyscraper. Most trees are flowering plants— the biggest, longest lived of all such plants. While most wildflowers live just a few years, some trees are thousands of years old. Trees often produce a huge number of blooms— called blossoms—for just a short time each year. Not all trees are flowering plants, however. Conifers like redwoods, and also cycads and ginkgos, make their seeds in cones, not flowers. They are called gymnosperms.

In spring, many fruit trees are covered briefly in delicately colored blossoms.

Roots, stems, and leaves

Did you know?
The roots of the South African wild fig tree penetrate 400 feet (120 m) below the ground.

Every flower has four main parts: roots, stem, leaves, and flowers. The flowers contain all the plant's reproductive parts. These are the parts that make the seeds. Flowers generally appear at certain stages in the plant's life. The roots, stem, and leaves are the green or brown parts, called the vegetative parts. They are there for all but the first few weeks of a plant's life.

The stem supports the plant's leaves and flowers. It is also a pipe through which water, minerals, and food move up and down between the roots and leaves. Water and minerals travel up through the stem from the roots through thin tubes called xylem. Food made in the leaves is carried to the rest of the plant in tubes called phloem.

Many plants have stems that are green and flexible. These are called herbaceous plants, because many, such as parsley, are herbs. Woody plants like trees and shrubs have stiff stems or trunks covered in bark.

Green leaves

Most leaves are colored green. They catch sunlight to make the food the plant needs to grow. Many leaves are broad and flat to catch as much sunlight as possible (see Food from light, pages 8–9). The lines on leaves are veins. Veins provide a framework to support the leaf. They also carry water in and the food the leaf makes out.

CLOSE-UP *Leaf structure*

Each leaf is attached to the stem by a small stalk, or petiole. The flat part of the leaf is called the blade. Some leaves, such as maple tree leaves are called simple leaves because they only have one blade. Other leaves, such as those of the walnut and willow tree, are called compound leaves because they have a number of blades on the same stalk.

ON THE TRACK *Counting petals*

Wildflowers are hard to recognize without their blooms. Once they are in flower, it becomes much easier. One clue to flower type is the number of petals.

flower detail

1. A red flower with many petals may be red clover. Other many-petaled flowers: indigo, lobelia, ladies' tresses, and plantain.

1

2. A white summer flower with 7 petals may be fleabane. There are many other 7-petal flowers: sunflower, coneflower, aster, and marsh marigold.

2

3. A blue summer flower with 6 petals may be pickerelweed. Other 6-petal flowers: pawpaw, bellwort, solomon's seal, and garlic.

4. A crimson flower with 3 petals is wake-robin. Other 3-petal flowers: wild ginger, little brown jug, heart-leaf, and trillium.

4

5. A white summer flower with 5 petals may be milkweed. There are many other 5-petal flowers: oxalis, yarrow, elderberry, comfrey, sorrel, agrimony, and blazing star.

5

6. A yellow spring flower with 4 petals may be evening primrose. Other 4-petal flowers: dodder, primrose willow, glade-cress, and Saint-John's-wort.

6

flower detail

Putting down roots

The roots are the parts of a plant that grow down into soil or water. Roots help hold the plant in place by anchoring it in the ground. They also draw up the water and minerals that the plant needs for growth. Some plants, such as beets, store food in their roots.

When a plant begins to grow, the seed sends out a single root called the primary root. This soon branches out into secondary roots. Some plants have just one large root, called a taproot, with just a few fine roots sprouting off it. Others, such as grasses, have lots of fine roots that spread out in a dense mat. These are called fibrous roots.

Did you know?

Some rye grasses can grow 7,000 miles of roots in just a cubic yard (14,000 km in a cubic meter) of soil.

Food from light

Unlike animals, plants make their own food by soaking up sunlight. Sun gives a plant energy to make a food called starch. To make starch, a plant uses two things: carbon dioxide from the air and water from the ground. It changes them in a process called photosynthesis. This occurs mainly in the leaves. Inside each cell are tiny packages called chloroplasts. These contain a green pigment (coloring) called chlorophyll. This substance is the key to photosynthesis, and is why leaves are usually green. The project here reveals how a leaf will not make any starch food if it is kept in the dark for long.

LEAVES IN THE DARK

You will need:

✔ Scissors
✔ Dark paper
✔ Denatured alcohol
✔ Small saucepan
✔ Iodine
✔ Hot water

✔ Small glass bowl
✔ Heat-proof measuring cup
✔ A dropper
✔ A houseplant

Did you know?

The biggest leaves of all belong to the raffia palm tree, which often grows leaves 65 feet (20 m) long.

1 Fold a piece of thick paper in half and tape it over one of the leaves of a plant. Leave the plant in a window for a week. Then pick the covered leaf and one that has not been covered.

2 Take one leaf by the end of its stalk and dip it in a shallow bowl of hot water from the faucet. Leave to soak for about a minute. Repeat the process with the other leaf with fresh hot water.

3 Pour about 4 fl oz (100 ml) of denatured alcohol into a measuring cup and stand it in a pan of water. Gently heat the pan until the spirits boil. Drop both leaves into the spirits and leave to cool.

4 When the spirits are cool and the leaves have turned white, put each leaf in a dish. Drip some iodine from a dropper over each leaf until it is completely covered.

Normal green untreated leaf

Normal leaf treated with iodine to reveal the presence of starch

Starved of light

A leaf needs light to make its food, called starch. Starch turns iodine black. If the leaf turns black with iodine, it shows that starch has been made. The leaf kept in the dark does not turn black. This shows that no starch has been made.

Take care

Make sure you have an adult to help you with the hot liquids. NEVER drink denatured alcohol.

Leaf kept in the dark shows no starch when treated with iodine

CLOSE-UP *Photosynthesis*

In photosynthesis, a leaf takes air in through tiny holes called stomata. It also takes water from the ground through the stem. The leaf's chlorophyll uses the sun's energy to split the water into hydrogen and oxygen. It then makes sugar by joining the hydrogen with carbon from carbon dioxide in the air. This sugar is the plant's food. It is carried through veins to where it is needed, while the waste oxygen is breathed out through the stomata. Around the plant, the sugar is converted into starches for storage, or burned up for energy. This process is called respiration.

Leaves soak up the sun's energy to make food for the plant to grow.

Plants and water

Plants depend on water. Without it, they soon die. Water fills every one of the tiny cells that make up each plant. Water helps keep the cells rigid, like air in a balloon. If the plant dries out, the cells collapse, and the plant wilts. Water is also a plant's transportation system. It carries dissolved gases, minerals, and nutrients where needed. Sometimes, the water streams up as sap through tubes in the stem. Sometimes, it just oozes from cell to cell through the cell walls. This process is called osmosis. Plants lose water all the time since it evaporates from the surfaces of leaves and flowers. As water is lost, more is sucked up through the stem to replace it. This project shows how water is drawn up through the stem even in cut flowers.

SEEING A FLOWER DRINK

You will need:

✔ Two tall glasses
✔ Craft knife
✔ Food coloring

✔ Carnations or similar cut flowers
✔ Tape

Did you know?
The desert-living rose of Jericho looks like a dead ball of twigs for years—then suddenly blooms when it rains.

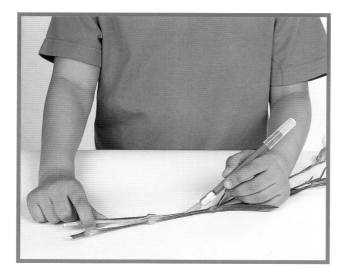

1 Ask an adult to help you slice the flower stem carefully in half lengthways with a craft knife. Take care to keep both halves neat and even. Stop when you get about halfway up the stem.

2 Take a piece of tape and wrap it several times around the stem at the end of the cut. This will prevent the stem splitting any farther. Lay the flowers gently to one side.

3 Fill two matching tall glasses with cold water. Add a few drops of food coloring to one of the glasses. The color does not matter, but blue or red look good.

Rising color
Carefully put each half of the stem in each glass. Place the glasses and flower in a sunny window, and leave to stand. Within a few hours, you might see traces of the food coloring appear in the flowers. After a day, the coloring should be very obvious. This shows that the water has been drawn up the stem and into the flower.

ON THE TRACK *Woodland flowers*

Where there is enough water for trees, there is enough for smaller flowers. Many woodland flowers bloom in spring. This way they catch the sun before it is blocked by the summer growth of leaves on the trees.

1. Also called wild sweet william, wild blue phlox appears in woods and fields from April to June.

2. The common blue violet is often candied and used in jellies.

3. Bloodroot gets its name from its red root, used as a dye by Native Americans.

4. Virginia bluebells look like blue carpets growing across damp woodland floors in eastern woods.

5. The wood lily is one of many thousands of lilies. This one is poisonous to animals, including people.

Did you know?
Window plants in deserts grow underground to save water. They have just a small green window on the surface to catch light.

Pollen and seeds

Did you know?
Bees collect pollen from flowers in the hairs on their legs, but some falls off on other flowers, and pollinates them.

A flower's task is to make seeds that can spread and grow into new plants. Just as there are male and female animals, a flower has male and female parts.

The male parts of a flower are called stamens. They make grains of pollen, which contain male sex cells. The female parts are called pistils, and they make eggs, or ovules, which are female sex cells. For a new plant to grow, a male sex cell needs to join an ovule. When that happens, the ovule is said to be fertilized. It then becomes a seed from which a new plant can grow.

The process begins when a pollen grain lands on the stigma of the same kind of flower. The stigma is the sticky patch on top of the pistil. Once pollen sticks to the stigma, it grows a tube down into the ovule to deliver its male sex cells. When that happens, the flower is said to be pollinated.

Spreading pollen

Some flowers are self-pollinating. This means the pollen moves from the stamens to the pistils of the same plant. Others are cross-pollinating. This means the pollen from the anther must be carried to the pistils of a different plant.

Some plants, such as grasses, rely on the wind to carry pollen. To help make sure that their pollen is caught on the breeze, grasses grow heads on tall stems that tower above other plants. Windblown pollen is tiny so

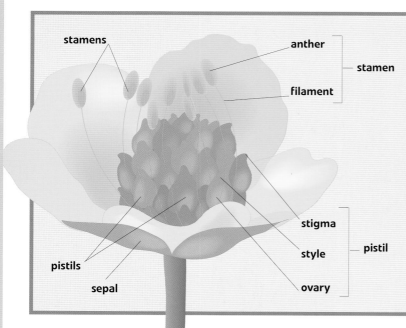

stamens
anther
stamen
filament
stigma
style
pistil
pistils
sepal
ovary

CLOSE-UP *Parts of a flower*

In the middle of most flowers are stubby green stalks called pistils. The pistils are the female parts of the flower. Flowers like buttercups have a clump of many pistils. Flowers like tulips have just one. Each pistil has a base called the ovary, where the flower's ovules are kept. Above the ovaries is a stalk called the style. This is topped by a sticky patch called the stigma which traps pollen. Arranged around the pistil, typically, are the spindly male parts, or stamens. Each stamen has a stalk called a filament topped by a head called an anther. Pollen is made at the anther in pollen sacs.

Swallowtail and flower
As it feeds on nectar, a swallowtail butterfly picks up some pollen. Some of this pollen will brush off on the next flower the butterfly visits.

that it will float on air. Single grains are visible only under a microscope, but big clouds can be seen. The chances of each grain landing on a stigma are small, but the plants make huge amounts of pollen. The plants also have big, feathery stigmas to catch pollen. Lots of pollen in the air can cause hay fever.

Other plants rely on insects, or even birds or bats, to carry their pollen. In tropical forests, for example, hummingbirds carry the pollen of certain flowers. Insect-pollinated plants have bigger, showier flowers than wind-pollinated plants. This helps them attract insects.

CLOSE-UP *Butterflies, bees, and moths*

Butterflies, bees, and moths play a key role in the lives of many flowers. Without such insects to carry their pollen from flower to flower, many plants would die out. Flowers have ways to attract their insect pollinators. These include bright colors, smells, and sweet sugary nectar, which the insects feed on. Bees use nectar to make honey. As an insect searches for nectar, pollen grains cling to its body, then rub off on the next flower it visits. Bees and butterflies are drawn to blue, yellow, purple, or pink flowers. Moths are drawn to white flowers that make their scent at night. A flower's petals form a landing platform for insects. Some petals have marks called honey guides. Like road signs, honey guides direct insects to the flower's nectar (and pollen-carrying stamens). Honey guides are often in ultraviolet (UV) colors. People cannot see the UV marks, but many insect pollinators can.

Did you know?
The football-sized white flower of the Amazon lily turns purple after it has been pollinated.

Spreading and growing

Once a flower has been pollinated, it can start to make the seeds from which a new plant can grow. When the pollen fuses with (fertilizes) the eggs in the flower's ovaries, the eggs start to change into seeds. The ovary begins to grow bigger around them. It forms what botanists (plant experts) call a fruit.

When botanists talk of fruit, they do not just mean oranges and lemons. They mean any ovary that contains developing seeds. As the seeds develop, the ovary swells around it. This swollen ovary is the plant's fruit. So every flowering plant grows fruit, not just fruit trees and berry bushes.

Many fruits are big, juicy, and sweet, like oranges. These are called soft fruits. The juicy flesh tempts animals to eat them, and this helps the plant. The seeds inside are too tough to digest, so they pass through the animal's gut intact and fall to the ground. In this way, the animals help spread the seeds—and add a little ready-made fertilizer.

Dry fruits

Dry and papery fruits can often manage without animals to spread them. Many dry seeds, such as poppies and orchids, are so small and light they can be blown far and wide by the wind alone. The feathery seed

Many shrubs make small fruits called berries that contain not just one seed but lots of small ones.

CLOSE-UP *True and false fruit*

Juicy fruits such as citrus fruit are sometimes called true fruits, because they are made from the ovary of the flower alone. Berries are true fruit made from a single ovary that contains lots of seeds. Apples and pears are called false fruits because they are made from more than just the ovary of the flower. The ovary is just the core, but the fleshy parts are swollen stalk. Fruits such as plums and cherries are called drupes. Drupes have a fleshy outside and a hard kernel or stone inside to protect the seeds. The stone may be too big for animals to swallow, so they eat just the flesh, but the seeds still get spread. Walnuts are also drupes. Peas and beans are really soft, dry fruits held in a case called a pod. Unlike most fruits they are not sweet.

Spreading seed
Grass produces huge amounts of seeds—all light and feathery enough to spread upon the wind.

cases of many grasses are especially light and carry huge distances on the breeze. Field maples, sycamores, and ash trees all have winged fruits called keys, that whirl on the wind like helicopters. Dandelions and thistle have parachutes of hairs to carry them along easily on the air.

Plants that live near streams often have dry seeds that can float away on the water. A few dry seeds, like burdocks, have burrs—hooks that catch on the fur of passing animals. Some dry fruits, like balsam, simply burst, which scatters seeds in all directions.

Hard nuts
Nuts, like Brazil nuts and hazelnuts, are really fruits. They are basically big seeds with a tough case, or shell. The shell is hard and dry, but the seed is soft enough and nourishing enough for animals to eat or bury as food stores. Squirrels bury hazelnuts in the ground to act as winter food stores. Since the squirrels only ever find a few of them again, the rest are placed nicely in the soil, ready to sprout in the spring.

Did you know?
Bananas, tomatoes, grapes, and cranberries are all different kinds of berries.

Growing from seeds

Seeds are little packages waiting to grow into a plant. Some seeds are tough and lay waiting to grow for years or even centuries. Most burst into life much quicker. As soons as it gets damp and warm enough, the seed starts to swell and split, and a root and a shoot emerge. The root, or radicle, grows down; the shoot, or plumule, grows up toward the sun and puts out tiny seed leaves, or cotyledons. Soon, the main stem and first true leaves appear. A young plant or seedling typically grows only at the tips of its roots and shoots. So at first, it grows longer rather than wider. This is called primary growth. Later, plants grow thicker and branch out. This project shows how you can grow sprouts (baby plants) from seeds in days.

GROWING SPROUTS

You will need:

✔ Watering can
✔ Cotton wool
✔ Scissors
✔ Two dishes

✔ Plant sprayer
✔ Garden cress seeds*
✔ Mustard seeds*

1 Cut a disk of cotton wool to fit each dish. You can use blotting paper instead. Lay a cotton wool disk gently inside each dish. Sprinkle water over them to dampen rather than soak them.

2 Sprinkle cress seeds evenly into one dish and mustard seeds into the other. Spray with water and leave in a warm, dark place. The seeds should burst and shoots appear overnight (inset).

* or alfalfa or mung beans

Tulips are typical monocots—fast growing, with soft stems and narrow leaves.

3 While your sprouts must not be soaked, they must never be allowed to dry out. So water them with a fine spray from a plant sprayer or watering can at least twice a day.

When a flowering plant grows from a seed, it sprouts either one or two seed leaves, or cotyledons. Seeds that sprout one leaf are called monocots (monocotyledons). Seeds that sprout two are dicots (dicotyledons). A quarter of all flowers—including grasses, cereals, daffodils, liles, and tulips—are monocots. They tend to grow quickly and stay soft and pliable. Their leaves are often narrow with parallel veins. Dicots such as trees often grow thicker and woodier. Their leaves tend to be broad with a network of veins. Monocots also develop a thick tangle of roots rather than one big one.

Early sprouts

Within a few days, the seeds are sending forth their seed leaves. After a week or so, the little mustard sprouts should be about an inch (2.5 cm) tall. The cress might take a little longer, but its leaves will be bigger. These seed leaves get their nourishment entirely from the seed. Plants draw their food from the soil and from sunlight only after they have grown true leaves and roots.

**Week-old
mustard sprouts**

**10-day-old
cress sprouts**

Through the years

Garden flowers and wildflowers all have their own flowering time. Each is adapted to flower at a certain time of year, typically early spring to late summer. Each also has its own life cycle. All flowering plants are divided into four basic types according to their life cycles: ephemerals, annuals, biennials, and perennials.

Short-lived flowers

Ephemerals are plants that grow from seed, bloom, and die in a few weeks. This can happen a few times in a season, so the plants can spread quickly. Many desert plants are ephemerals. Annuals are plants that grow from seed, spread their seeds, and die in a single growing season. Seeds may lie in the ground for years before conditions are right for growing. Many herbs, peas, and cereals are annuals.

CLOSE-UP *Spreading without seeds*

Perennials do not make many seeds but spread by growing shoots from roots or stems. This is called vegetative propagation. Irises sprout from a thick underground stem, or rhizome. Potatoes grow from a thick rhizome end called a tuber. Crocuses grow from a bulbous stem base, or corm. Tulips grow from bulbs, made from layers like the layers of an onion. Many plants spread by growing long stems that creep over the ground (runners) or under it (suckers).

ON THE TRACK *Prairie wildflowers*

In spring and summer, the prairie blooms with colorful flowers. Most are perennials.

1. Blooming from May to July, Indian paintbrushes often get extra food and water by tapping their roots into those of other plants.

2. The distinctive, drooping ray petals of the prairie coneflower appear from May to August.

3. Named for its resemblance to a girl's bonnet, the bluebonnet flowers bloom in early spring.

4. The prairie goldenrod blooms in late summer. It has very deep roots.

5. The sunflower blooms in late summer. It turns its head to follow the sun.

6. The pasqueflower gets its name because it blooms at Easter. *Pasque* is French for "Easter."

Long-lived flowers

Biennials last for two years. In the first summer, the young plant sends energy from its leaves into an underground food store such as a root or bulb. This sustains it through winter. Leaves and flowers often die off. The next spring, it sends up a stem that flowers in the summer. Many vegetables, such as carrots, are biennials. So are foxgloves, carnations, and evening primroses.

Perennials survive at least three years. They get through the winter with a bulb or similar underground food store. They may not bloom in the first year, but bloom every year after. Primroses, asters, irises, lupines, and peonies are perennials.

Mountain perennials

Mount Rainier in the Cascade Range in Washington State is famous for its lupines. These perennials survive the cool mountain winters by storing food in the old stem over winter. Then they regrow in spring.

Flower colors

Flowers come in many colors and hues, from delicate blue violets to red roses. The colors are not just for show. They have evolved to attract the insects and birds that pollinate the plants. Red flowers, like Indian paintbrushes and California fuchsia, attract butterflies and hummingbirds. Blue lupines and yellow coneflowers attract bees. White flowers are easy to see in dim light. They attract flies in a gloomy wood, or moths at night. The colors in flowers come from pigments (chemical colorings). These pigments are called anthocyadins. Blue-violet flowers, for instance, contain an anthocyadin called delphinidin, after the delphiniums it was first found in. This project shows how to find out the different combinations of pigments in flowers.

FINDING PLANT PIGMENTS

You will need:

✔ Variety of flowers
✔ Glasses or jars
✔ Pencils
✔ Pestle and mortar

✔ Nail polish remover
✔ Blotting paper
✔ Stapler
✔ Teaspoon

1 Collect a variety of flowers. Strip the flower petals off each. Then take the petals of one kind and put them in the mortar with four teaspoons of nail polish remover. Take care not to spill any.

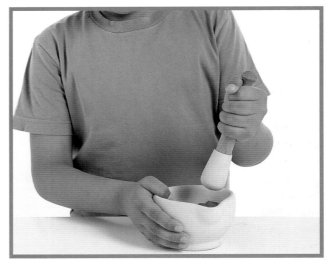

2 Using the pestle, firmly grind the mix of petals and nail polish remover until it all becomes a mush. This may take ten minutes or more. Pore the liquid into a glass.

3 Staple a strip of blotting paper around a pencil and rest the pencil on the top of the glass so that the blotting paper just dips into the liquid at the bottom of the glass.

CLOSE-UP *Roses*

Roses are among the most popular of all garden flowers because of their lovely perfume and beautiful blooms. Over the centuries, gardeners have managed to produce a huge variety of rose colors, from blue to peach. Wild roses usually have small flowers and a single layer of five petals. Garden roses have bigger flowers with multiple sets of five petals in two or more layers. There are 100 species of wild roses. But all 13,000 of today's garden roses were created by crossing just 10 wild Asian species. Some experts divide garden roses according to the time they bloom. "Old" roses, such as yellow briars, damasks, and many climbing roses, bloom once a year in early summer. "Perpetual" roses bloom twice: once in early summer, then again in fall. "Everblooming" roses, such as floribundas, gloribundas, and polyanthas, bloom all summer. "Hybrid tea" roses, such as the Peace, were created by crossing fragile everblooming tea roses with vigorous perpetual roses.

Split colors
After an hour or so, the nail polish remover, together with the pigments, has traveled up the blotting paper. Different pigments will travel a different distance. They separate to form what is called a chromatograph. Leave the blotting paper to dry and then repeat the experiment with different petals.

Did you know?
More than half of all the world's cut flowers are grown in the Netherlands in Europe.

Where flowers live

Did you know?
The Australian water plant wolffia duckweed is the world's smallest flower, just 0.02 inches (0.6 mm) across.

Each kind of wildflower has its own favorite place to live. Some need hot, dry climates. Others like to live in cold, damp places. Each kind of place has its own unique range of wildflowers.

Woodlands and prairies

Woodlands are homes for plants that prefer shady conditions under the trees to full sunlight. In spring, flowers such as bluebells and primroses bloom quickly before the leaves have grown dense on the trees. Violets, phlox, and willow herb manage to flower into summer by growing in clearings and by streams. Other woodland flowers are shown on page 11.

Grasslands look dull from a distance, but a close look reveals a huge range of plants. Hundreds of kinds of grass grow in the prairies, for instance. On the high, dry western plains, short grasses like buffalo and blue grama grow. Farther east is a mix of grasses such as June and needle grass. Farther east still, where it is moister, tall grasses, such as Indian grass and big blue stem, grow. Among the grasses bloom a huge range of flowers that like full sunlight and can take drier conditions. These include goldenrod, which finds moisture with deep roots, and Indian paintbrush, which taps other plants for moisture. Other prairie flowers are shown on page 19.

CLOSE-UP *Desert flowers*

With so little water, deserts are perhaps the toughest of all places for plants to survive. Yet many plants have found ways to cope. Some plants, like mesquite, have very long roots for finding moisture deep underground. Others have developed thick, waxy leaves to cut down evaporation. Among the most impressive of the desert survivors, though, are cactuses. Cactuses have no leaves and a very thick skin. This keeps water loss down. Their fat stems can also hold huge amounts of water, which is why they are sometimes called succulents. Such lush vegetation is rare in the desert. So plants like cactuses, prickly pears, and thornbushes have thorns and spikes to protect against animals.

Tumbleweed grows in many American desert regions.

Water lilies
The leaves of water lilies are so big and flat they float on the water. But their long stalks reach down to the riverbed so the roots are firmly anchored.

Mountains and wetlands

The weather gets colder, windier, and wetter in higher areas, so plants that grow on mountains must be hardy. On lower slopes big trees may grow. But higher up, there are only low grasses and mats of tiny flowers such as blue columbine and moss pink. High mountain plants have evolved various ways of coping with the cold. Some have a coat of woolly hairs. Others have thick waxy leaves that do not freeze easily.

The very first plants developed in water, then moved to the land. Many plants, though, have adapted to live in damp places or in water. These include water lilies and water hyacinths, and grasslike plants such as reeds and rushes. Some, like pickerelweed, root in pond beds. Others, such as cattails and arrowheads, grow on the banks. Monkey flowers and others grow along streams.

Did you know?
The leaves of the giant Amazon lily are 6 feet (1.8 m) across and can support a child's weight.

Plant responses

The way a plant grows depends on what kind of plant it is and the conditions around it. Every plant cell contains chemical instructions, called genes, inherited from its parent plants. One way genes control the way the plant grows is by sending out chemicals called hormones. When cells send out the hormone called gibberellin, for instance, the plant knows it is time to flower.

Plants also respond to the conditions around them. Because they need light to live, they often bend toward light. This bending is called phototropism. They also bend with gravity, to make sure stems grow upward and roots grow down. This is called geotropism. This project shows both these kinds of tropism in action.

TROPISM IN ACTION

You will need:

✔ Broad-bean seeds
✔ Potting compost

✔ Plastic cups
✔ Plant sprayer

Did you know?
Sunflowers and other flowers are "heliotropic," which means they turn toward the sun as it moves through the sky.

1 Soak two bean seeds thoroughly in water overnight. Fill two plastic cups with compost, and press one seed vertically a little way into the compost in each cup. Water each day for a week.

2 When shoots appear, put them on a window sill. When they are 2 inches (5 cm) tall, lay one cup on its side. Leave for another three days, tipping it upright again briefly each day for watering.

ON THE TRACK *Roadside flowers*

Tropism ensures plants make the most of conditions they find—and many flowers adapt well to roadside conditions. In North America, many roadside flowers are originally from Europe. These include dandelion, Saint-John's-wort, chicory, and burdock.

1. Chicory flowers open with the sun in the morning and close again about midday. If the weather is cloudy, only a few flowers open. Dried and roasted chicory is used to flavor coffee.

2. Burdock flower heads are covered in hooklike burrs that stick to clothing and animal fur. In this way, the flower is spread over large areas.

3. Dandelions get their name from the French for lion's teeth, *dents de lion*, because of their toothed leaves.

4. Fireweed gets its name because it springs up in areas that have been burned. It helps stablize soil, then dies back as other plants return.

5. Saint-John's-wort's name might come from a legend that a red oil was collected from its flowers on Saint John's Day, June 24. The red was said to represent the blood of the beheaded saint.

3 After three days or so, you should find the stem has started to bend and grow upward as it responds to gravity. This is geotropism in action. It works because the plant is told to grow by hormones called auxins that ooze from the tip of the stem. When the plant is on its side, the auxins ooze down mainly into the lower side of the stem. Responding to the extra auxins, the lower side of the stem grows more than the top side and so bends the stem upward.

Light response

With the second bean plant, you can try phototropism in action—that is, bending to the light. Move the plant away from the window, and turn it so that it leans away from the window. Within a day, the stem should have twisted back toward the window. Like geotropism, this happens because of auxins. Light keeps auxins from working, so they cause less growth on the side of the stem facing the light. This makes the plant bend over.

Did you know?

Some plants, like insect-eating Venus's flytraps (page 27), can make movements faster than any animal.

Unusual plants

Did you know?
The bladderwort is a water plant that has tiny bags on its roots. The bags trap the water insects the plant feeds on.

Garden flowers and wildflowers with colorful blooms are by no means the only plants. There are a host of much more extraordinary looking plants.

Flowers have many ways to attract the birds and insects that pass on their pollen. They also grow into all kinds of different shapes. Bee orchids look so much like female bees that male bees try to mate with them. Titan arums, on the other hand, attract their pollinators in a very different way. Titan arums have a smell so like rotting meat that flies love them.

Giant flowers

Titan arums are the world's tallest flowers. They can grow more than 8 feet (2.5 m) tall. They live in the forests of Sumatra and flower very rarely. When specimens in the New York Botanical Garden and in the Royal Botanical Gardens at Kew in London come into flower, it is a major news event.

Even more unusual than the Titan arum is the world's biggest and heaviest flower, rafflesia. This flower grows in the jungles of Borneo and Sumatra. It is a parasite, which means it steals food from other plants. It has no leaves, stem, or proper roots. It is a single flower more than 3 feet (1 m) across and weighing more than 14 pounds (7 kg). Rafflesia blooms just four days a year.

Pitcher plant
There are at least 70 species of pitcher plants. They all have vaselike pitchers that hang from thin stems called tendrils. Any insect that falls in is doomed.

CLOSE-UP *Orchids*

Orchids are one of the biggest families of flowers. Many are among the most distinctive of all flowers. There more than 20,000 kinds of orchids, from tiny plants 0.25 inches (0.6 cm) across to vines 100 feet (30 m) long. Most live in warm tropical areas. Some are widespread, while others may grow in just a single valley on a single mountain in the world. Many orchids grow on the trunks or branches of trees, or on rocks, rather than in the soil like other flowers. These orchids are called epiphytes. A few, such as the bird's nest orchid, live off rotting plants and do not need light like all other plants. These are called saprophytes. Orchid flowers all have a big central petal called the lip, or labellum. It is often shaped like a cup, trumpet, or bag. But nearly every orchid depends on one particular insect, bird, or bat to pollinate it. The orchid's lip is often shaped to attract its own animal pollinator. Some orchids attract their pollinator by mimicking it. The fly orchid has a lip shaped like a female tachinid fly to attract male flies. Others actually trap the insect in the flower.

Bee orchids look so like female bees that male bees try to mate with them and get covered in pollen.

Flesh eaters

Even more extraordinary than plants that smell like meat are plants that eat meat. Plants like these get their food by digesting animal flesh, usually insects. They are called carnivorous plants. There are more than 500 species. One is the Venus's flytrap which has jaws that snap shut on insects in an instant. Others include giant pitcher plants that swallow frogs, rats, or even birds.

With the Venus's flytrap, insects are lured into the jaws with nectar. As the insect lands, the jaws clamp shut. The plant then oozes juices that drown, then dissolve the trapped insect. A week later, the insect is digested, and the trap opens again.

The leaves of the carnivorous sundew plant are covered in tentacles that ooze drops of a sticky substance called mucilage. The mucilage gives the plant its name, because it glistens in the sun like dew. When an insect lands on the mucilage, it gets stuck. As it struggles to get free, the sundew's tentacles go into action. In ten seconds, the tentacles have wrapped around the insect and suffocated it with slime.

Did you know?

Vanilla flavoring comes from vinelike vanilla orchids that grow in Mexico and elsewhere in the tropics.

Identifying flowers

There are about 250,000 different species (kinds) of flowers. So when you see one in the wild, it can be hard to figure out which flowering plant it is. But you can begin to identify it by looking at the shape of its blooms.

When looking at the shape of a flower, you will see that many grow in clusters, like milkweed. These clusters are inflorescences. With some flowers, like snapdragons, you can easily see the individual flowers in the cluster. With others, like asters, burdocks, daisies, and dandelions, each inflorescence looks like a single flower. The shape of this cluster gives you a clue to which group of flowers the plant belongs. The cluster can be any one of the three shapes listed below. Regular, trumpet, and bell-shaped flowers can be identified from single blooms.

 Composite flowers

 Rounded clusters

 Elongated clusters

 Regular flowers

 Irregular flowers

Trumpet or bell-shaped flowers

COMPOSITE FLOWERS

With composite flowers, the individual flowers look like petals of a single flower.

ID clues:
- Lots of narrow petals, often in layers.
- Flowers often have no stalk but grow from a head at the tip of the flower stem.
- Each flower is long and narrow. Looks rather like a single petal.

New England aster: Family COMPOSITAE/ASTERACEAE
Asters, daisies, and dandelions belong to the vast family called Asteraceae, with more than 20,000 species. All have flower heads with raylike florets (miniflowers), each with a single narrow petal. The flower head is surrounded by leaflike structures called bracts.
Garden asteraceae: *Aster, dahlia, chrysanthemum, artichoke, lettuce*
Wildflower asteraceae: *Burdock, thistle, ragweed, sagebrush, butter burr, dandelion*

Dandelion: Family COMPOSITAE/ASTERACEAE
Dandelions have raylike yellow flower heads, with up to 200 florets. Unusually, the ovaries of the flowers form fertile seeds without pollen. The head turns to a mass of feathery hairs, ready to spread the seeds on the wind.
Similar flowers: *Hawks head, hawks beard*

Oxeye daisy: Family COMPOSITAE/ASTERACEAE
The oxeye daisy has white florets and a yellow center. It comes originally from Eurasia, but is now widespread in North America.
Similar flowers include: *May weed, fleabane*

ROUNDED CLUSTERS

The flowers are entirely separate, but grouped in rounded clusters.

ID clues:
- Tiny but clearly separate flowers in clusters.
- The clusters are on long thin stalks.

Phlox: Family POLEMONIACEAE
Phloxes are low-growing flowers that creep across woodland floors. They have five triangular petals mounted on a trumpet shape. Wild phloxes include the wild blue phlox and fall phlox. Garden phloxes are either creeping phlox or moss phlox.
Similar flowers: *Periwinkle, myrtle*

Saint-John's-wort: Family HYPERICACEAE
Saint-John's-worts belong to a family of 350 low-growing herbs and shrubs related to tropical tea trees, including Aaron's beard and Saint Andrew's cross. Most have yellow flowers with five petals.
Similar flowers: *Tinker's penny, Saint Peter's wort*

Parsley: Family APIACEAE
Parsley belongs to a huge family of scented herbs with feathery leaves and a white, flat-topped cluster of flowers, or umbel. The family includes Queen Anne's lace and carrots.
Similar flowers: *Hemlock, cow parsnip, yarrow*

Clover: Family FABACEAE
Clovers belong to the huge pea family, Fabaceae. They are small, fragrant flowers with three (rarely four) leaflets on each leaf. They include red clover and shamrock. Clover comes from Eurasia, but was imported to North America to improve hay crops.
Similar flowers: *Silver leaf locoweed, field milkwort*

Forget-me-not: Family BORAGINACEAE
These belong to the borage family and have a cluster of blue flowers. Their name comes from the legend of a knight who fell in a river as he picked flowers for his lady. As he drowned, he said, "Forget-me-not."
Similar flowers: *Sky pilot, blue-eyed grass*

ELONGATED CLUSTERS

The flowers are separate, but grouped in long, often spikelike clusters.

ID clues:
- Tiny but clearly separate flowers in clusters.
- Long spike of flowers.

Wild lupine: Family FABACEAE
There are 200 different kinds of lupine. They live mainly on the North American prairies and by the Mediterranean in Europe. They are tall flowers with an upright spike, typically white or blue. They include the Texas bluebonnet.
Similar flowers: *Purple loco, hairy vetch*

Canada goldenrod: Family ASTERACEAE
Goldenrods are tall flowers, with yellow spiked flower heads and toothed leaves. They are found almost everywhere in eastern North America. They once bloomed in huge numbers on the Great Plains.
Similar flowers: *Lance-leaved goldenrod, seaside goldenrod*

Giant paintbrush: Family SCROPHULARIACEAE
Paintbrushes belong to the snapdragon family, which have tube-shaped flowers in clusters. They include speedwell and foxgloves. Paintbrushes get their name from the way the tops of their flowers look as if they have been dipped in red, orange, yellow, pink, or white paint. They are parasitic plants that feed on the roots of other plants.
Similar flowers: *Indian paintbrush*

Purple loosestrife: Family PRIMULACEAE
Purple loosestrife has tapered spikes of purple flowers. They were introduced from Eurasia to North America where they are now a weed.
Similar flowers: *Blazing star, fireweed*

Pickerelweed: Family PONTEDERIACEAE
Pickerelweed are water flowers with blue spikes.
Similar flowers: *Water hyacinth, plantain*

29

REGULAR FLOWERS

Many flowers are completely symmetrical, with a ring of identical petals.

ID clues:
- Each flower has its own stalk.
- Seven or less petals on each flower.

Common buttercup: Family RANUNCULEAE
Buttercups are small, glossy, yellow flowers with five petals. They grow in woods and fields everywhere and belong to a huge family called the buttercup or Ranunculeae family.
Similar flowers: *Marsh marigold, anemone, pasqueflower*

Large-flowered trillium: Family LILIACEAE
With their three big petals and three big leaves, trilliums earn their name, which is Latin for "three." They belong to the huge lily family, which also includes bluebells, tulips, and hyacinths.
Similar flowers: *Purple trillium, western wake robin, water lily*

Evening primrose: Family ONAGRACEAE
Evening primroses make up a huge family of American plants, nearly all with four petals. Like its European namesake, the primrose, the evening primrose is yellow. It opens at dusk to be pollinated by night-flying moths.
Similar flowers: *Fireweed, enchanter's nightshade*

California poppy: Family PAPAVERACEAE
Poppy flowers, like the California poppy, are vivid orange, red, purple, or yellow, with four to six big petals like tissue paper. The flowers often last just one day, but a single poppy plant may produce 400 or more in a season.
Similar flowers: *Rose mallow, corn cockle*

Rugosa rose: Family ROSACEAE
Roses came originally from Asia, but they now grow all around the world. They are mostly woody shrubs or trees, and usually have thorned stems.
Similar flowers: *Bramble, blackberry*

IRREGULAR FLOWERS

Some flowers, including orchids, are made from different petal shapes.

ID clues:
- Each flower has its own stalk.
- Petals are different shapes.

Canada violet: Family VIOLACEAE
Violets are small, low shrubs, usually with blue, purple, white, or yellow flowers. Flowers have two pairs of different petals and a smaller spur petal.
Similar flowers: *Pansy, dog violet*

Blue flag: Family IRIDACEAE
Named after the Greek goddess of the rainbow, irises like blue flag come in many colors. They have three bent back petals and three smaller upright ones.
Similar flowers: *Red iris, yellow flag*

TRUMPETS AND BELLS

Some flowers have small or large trumpet-, bell-, and funnel-shaped flowers.

ID clues:
- Each flower has its own stalk.
- The flower forms a complete cup shape.

Common morning glory: Family CONVOLVULACEAE
Morning glories grow on twining vines and have beautiful, funnel-shaped flowers that open for just a few hours after dawn.
Similar flowers: *Bindweed, jimsonweed, sweet potato*

Harebell: Family CAMPANULACEAE
Harebells have delicate light blue flowers that hang like bells from fine stems. They belong to a huge family of bell-shaped flowers, the Campanulaceae.
Similar flowers: *Bellflower, Virginia bluebell*

Glossary

angiosperm Flowering plant, a plant that makes its seeds with flowers.

annual Plant that grows from seed, flowers, and dies in a single year.

anther The top of the stamen (the male part of a flower) where pollen is made.

anthocyadins Chemical colorings in plants.

biennial Plant that grows from seed one year and flowers the next.

chlorophyll The green substance in plants that captures the sun's energy.

chloroplast Cell containing chlorophyll.

conifer Tree that makes its seeds in cones.

dicot Plant that grows two seed leaves.

ephemeral Plant that grows from seed and then flowers, usually briefly, at various times.

epiphyte Plant that grows on top of another plant but does not draw anything from it.

filament Stalk that supports an anther.

fruit The swollen ovary of a flower after it has been pollinated and begins to grow seeds.

gymnosperm Plant that makes seeds in cones.

monocot Plant starting with one seed leaf.

nectar The sweet liquid made by flowers to attract the insects and birds that pollinate them.

osmosis Slow oozing between plant cells of liquids containing dissolved chemicals.

ovary Part of a flower that makes eggs. It turns into a fruit containing seeds after pollination.

ovule Egg that will turn into a seed.

perennial Plant that flowers year after year.

petiole The stalk of a leaf.

phloem Tubes in a plant's stem that carry food.

photosynthesis The way leaves use the sun's energy to make sugar from air and water.

pistil The female part of a flower, containing an ovary where eggs are made.

pollen Tiny packages containing a plant's male sex cells.

radicle The part of a seed that forms the root.

seed leaf Leaf that sprouts straight from a seed.

stamens The male parts of a flower that make pollen.

starch A plant's sugary food.

stigma The top of the female parts of a flower, where pollen is caught.

stomata Tiny pores in a leaf.

taproot Large single root.

tropism How a plant grows to follow gravity, light, and other factors.

vegetative propagation How a plant spreads without seeds by growing new plants from the roots or stem.

FURTHER READING:
David Burnie. *Plant*. New York, NY: Alfred A. Knopf, 1989.

Susan Hood. National Audubon *First Field Guide, Wildflowers*. New York, NY: Scholastic, 1998.

Jack Sanders. *Hedgemaids and Fairy Candles*. Camden, ME: Ragged Mountain Press, 1995.

Richard Spellenberg. National Audubon *Pocket Guide to Familiar Flowers of North America*. New York, NY: Alfred A. Knopf, 1994.

Index